Joy Yet Resides Here

also by VK Press

Dating Daddy
Realizing God as Father through Daddy Issues and Bad
Romance
Shavonne L. Holton

Bursting at the Seams
A Collection of Poetry
Chantel Massey

nomaD
januarie York

Suffer Well
Poems for the Grieving
Korie Griggs

Joy Yet Resides Here

Candace Boyd Simmons

VK PRESS

Indianapolis, IN

VK Press, LLC
PO BOX 78044
Indianapolis, IN 46278
www.vkpresses.com

Editor: Januarie York
Design: ess mckee
Illustrations: Tanía Michelle Wineglass

Library of Congress Control Number: 2024915505

First edition published May 20, 2025
in the United States by VK Press, LLC

E-Book ISBN 979-8-9911088-0-5
Paperback ISBN 979-8-9911088-1-2

To my littlest love, Maddie:

You were a dream. God knew I'd be born anew in birthing
you. What a gem you are. Mama loves you, BIGLY.
Thank you for a love like yours.
Life is much sweeter with you in it.

To the lover of my heart, SMBS:

It has been your prayers. It has been your laughter.
It has been your tears. It has been the beauty of your faith
that has dug me out and drawn me back in.
Love, always. All ways.

For me:

You can. And you will. And you do.
For you. Always.
God is with her. She can not fail.

Table of Contents

Foreword

Isn't it interesting how love exists in full without grief, but that grief is merely a reflection of abundant love made homeless? We don't define the act or the feeling of love by how much grief we can consume. When given and received properly, it feels like a walk-through infinite space with floral paved futures. Grief, on the other hand, IS love. It's what happens when a story we hoped to outlive ends, and the love becomes homeless, but not lifeless; helpless, but no less abundant. Grief is all the love you have for a thing coming to the realization that it can no longer be properly distributed to its original host.

To lament is to love.

I never met Patrice, but I remember the fall of 2021. Specifically, I recall Candace, as she publicly slid on the shoes of the mourning and laced her feet in devastation. I could tell her spirit had been rocked to its core and I recognized her mourning – it hit differently. It was a lament I knew all too well. Grief is only ever understood by the experience of being thrust into a relationship with it. It's both powerful and relentless and can cause you to question your ability to recover. They say there are 6 stages to grieving, but I've personally always found 5 and 6 (acceptance and moving on) the hardest to advance to. Denial, anger, bargaining, and depression will sit with you.

They will sit,
with you. Everywhere you sit.

Touching every part of you. Interrupting your routines and creating moments of despair, panic, and anxiety. It's a never-ending party that you're not quite sure how you got to or if you're even dressed for, but there's no ride back to before it began.

The floor beneath you feels like it's caving in while the sky above seems too quiet. It's unreasonable. Is anyone even up there?

"You don't have anything to say about this?"

"No messages you want to send? Wow God. Just wow."

Even the most hardened, angered, questioning Christian knows two things are true – God is love and it is God's comfort through time and prayer that will help us advance through stages. Now, if grief and God are both love, then shouldn't God be able to handle our grief, even when it's full of questions?

In the 1991 John Singleton movie *Boyz in the Hood*, after the murder of his brother Ricky, character Doughboy says, *"I just feel like he punched the wrong clock on Rick tho,"* in reference to God making no mistakes. But even with our teachings and beliefs, isn't it at least fair to question God? To feel like a mistake was made? When grief has us spinning out of control, we should be able to turn to God with all that we feel and trust that comfort, peace, and love will meet us there.

Candace's grief was palpable in a relatable way. I remembered my personal one on one time with grief, which was as fresh as two years prior, so feeling her pain was easy. When this type of grief stands in front of you, words, thoughts, and even prayers can all be moot points. The throughway is painful and there is nothing to make it easier. *Joy is a right that is earned through our tears.*

Our human experiences produced with this book is an inside look at her private relationship with God and how grief, humans, and life itself can spark everything from distance to desire. These pages hold an outpouring of emotions and stillness where there are questions.

Be reminded that God's love is not restrictive and capturing joy is your right. God will take care of us and usher us right back to where joy resides. Candace takes us along her journey of keeping at least one finger in God's hand, one hand holding joy, and one heart full of love. The book in its entirety is a prayer given while searching for answers and holding tight to love. Where there is love, joy may reside, *and reside well.*

Januarie York, Poet
Author of *nomaD*

Preface

Joy and lamenting? a shaky Christian.

That sounds cool, but what does that mean?

I'm glad you asked.

Inside you will find prayers that I lift up to a good, kind and loving God.

A God who never waivers. A God who always hears.

Even in their *silence*.

The laments are to that same God. Some of the laments feel like questions, because what is a faith that doesn't ask questions?

The joys are here too. They remind me just how interconnected we really are.

a note: I talk to God like God is a friend, because if I can't be real with and to God, what does all this mean?

I know I've been kept and covered and deeply loved by God.

I know grief tried to swallow me whole, but I persisted and allowed my joy and my grief to hold hands.

I know that I wrote things and spoke things and they became so.

I know the woman I married sees me and in her seeing, she knows me more than I thought possible.

I know I watched an amazing 9 year old blossom and bloom. She's going to take this world by storm and I hope y'all are ready.

I know that I found God in the strangest places and ways.

I'm thankful for the beauty.

I know for every win, I experienced a loss or three.

But lessons and blessings go hand and hand.

This is what happens when a shaky Christian who still believes lays it all bare for and to a God who never stops showing up.

Introduction

As a young girl growing up in church, my pastor would eloquently begin every sermon with a prayer from Psalms 19:14, "May the words of my mouth, and the meditation of my heart, be pleasing in your sight, Oh, Lord, my strength and my redeemer." This grew to be a prayer I would pray often, especially as I wrote this book. I needed God to be my strength. I needed God to redeem me, even from the mess of self. As I started this book of prayers and laments, I echoed these same words, but with an added notion.

Dear Reader, let these meditations, written from my heart, provide balm for the storm. May you gleam from them what I have from God, who has been and will always be my strength and my redeemer.

Joy yet resides here.

Prologue

I'm wrestling with it. Still. Almost three years later at the time of this writing. It's hard. I've asked God, "Why her?"a million times over.

You were loved by many. A friend to many. A supporter of countless. Mama. Daughter. Sister. Fashionista. Music head.

All of that and so much more. But to me- you were MY cousin. My Tricie.

We had just been together and yet unbeknownst to me, weeks later, you would be promoted to ancestor.

But that day, we laughed, cried, and danced to PJ Morton.

You zipped me up and prepped me to go join my love.

How kind of God to let us love you.

How caring of God to send us a sweet light in you.

How selfish of God to want you back.

God let light be glorified through your life, your work, and your children.

Some people go their entire lives without having a Patrice. But I was loved well by you.
We all were.

Even in my grief, my heart sings, "How kind of God."

I'll love you, forever.

I love you more. I love you more. I love you more.

The Prayers

prayer

[prair]

noun

1. an act of thanksgiving, supplication, sometimes you
   leave your confessions too.

2. a time of communion with God or a being worthy of
   worship.

Prayer is My Way of Communing and Connecting with God

I speak with God when I wake, dress, and, even when I drive.

God and I talk.

My prayers are a conversation.

Sometimes I speak.

Sometimes I listen.

Always, we commune.

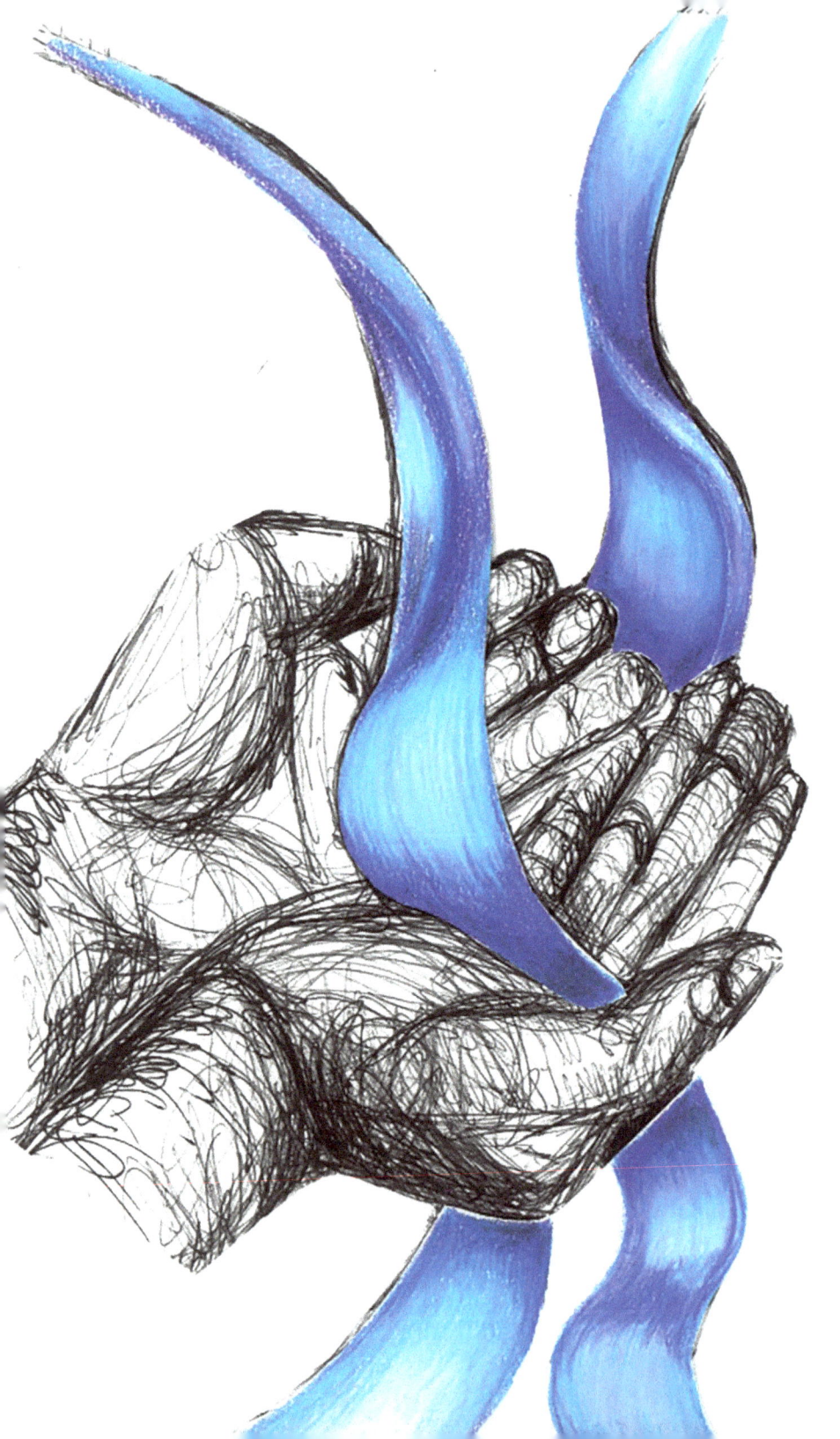

A Daily Prayer

My daily prayer: God, go before me.
Be where I need you to be.
Abide in me.
Amen.

A Love Like Yours

God, we ask for grace.

God, we ask for mercy.

But most of all, we ask for a love like yours.

A Prayer of Thanks for Friendship

For the truth tellers.

> the *friend* that leans in and gives you truth when you need it most.

For the truth holders.

> the *lover* that knows the secrets and how to handle them.

For the burden bearers.

> the *sister* who holds your hand and insures you it will bc ok.

For the friends.

The real ones.

For the gift of loving you with all your stuff.

We give thanks.

The Art of the Return

Let the heart that yearns to laugh, return to itself.
Let the mind that yearns to calm, return to itself.
Amen.

Cracks

God, I see you!

Repairing cracks and making ways better aligned and slightly easier to travel.

Because the paths and people are not always straight nor smooth,

restoring the joys and proving how good indeed you are.

Because life gets hard and takers will make you think nothing good can come from your faith.

But God,

I see you.

God, I hear you.

God, I feel you.

It's for these things and the more.

The more of You and Your presence that I am thankful for,

Immensely.

But What If They Do?

For babies grown and nourished in bruised and seemingly
infertile wombs.

Oh, that they will come forth.

With breath in their lungs.

Filled with God's joy and majesty.

We give thanks to the Creator of something out of nothing.

For springs in dry deserts.

For removal of dust on dry bones.

God, we thank you.

What a Friend

Like the dew in the morning. Rest upon me, O' God.
I am in mourning.
The deaths.
The doors closed.
The no's and not yet's.
The backs turned.
God, be a friend.
Restore hope.
Amen.

Joy Yet Resides Here

For the Many

For cousins,
For coffee coated conversations,
For good eats,
For sisterhood,
For villages,
For those who love your preschooler like their own,
For those who give respite,
We give thanks.

God is Among Them

Black women save my life daily.

And that's on Mary, her son, who is the lamb.

A fish dinner.

Fly finger waves and some bomb hoop earrings.

Long glitter nails and nose rings.

Glossy red lips with the purse to match.

Black women are God's embodiment of all things good.

God is among them.

Dreams Not Yet Deferred

God of my wildest dreams.

Help me to remember that it won't always feel like this.

Remind me through your unwavering love that broken fences can be mended.

Recall to me that you are the joy of my strength.

Help me to seek your face.

Even when your voice feels faint.

Restore the hope I once held

> that YOU
>
> are still the source
>
> and a constant friend,
>
> an always present help.
>
> God dreams don't happen without you.
>
> Remind me of who I am in You.

I Believe You to Be So

Oh God, Our Father, Our Mother, Our Sister too
Our gathering place.
Our protector and provider.
Be with us today.
Give us joy today.
Give us strength today.
Revive us again.
Remind us, you're THE source.
Remind us, you're THE plug.
Remind us, you're THE one.
Mender. Fixer. Way maker.
We believe it to be so.
Amen.

A Selah Praise

From the fruit of my lips
From the deepest depths of my heart
I offer a selah praise.
In all things
Good and bad.
Things promised and those yet unseen.

If the Gifts May Come

They say that gifts come without repentance.
They are God given and
for these things, we are thankful.
Amen.

All to Know You More

Your word is a light.

For the pathways that are dark and lovely and lonely.

May your grace meet us there.

All to know you more.

Remind me to stay focused on You.

Knowing that I can come to you in all ways with all things.

All to know you more.

Remind me that in my query- you may not answer urgently.
It's my urgency that calls on you loudly.

All to know you more.

Remind me that you are freedom.

Knowing You is this freedom.

Amen.

For the Things We Know to Be True

For answered prayers.

For moments of waiting.

For love everlasting.

For lessons.

For laughter.

For stillness.

It's in these things that I knew your voice.

It was those nights that I felt your care.

It is these things that I know You to be true.

The Many Ways You've Made

There are times when I'm in awe of the stages and platforms God lays before me.

And then I remember my prayers.

Sometimes I couldn't fall asleep and I prayed for a peaceful rest.

And then I remember the calling.

It was in the moments of doubt and imposter syndrome where it felt like this weight was too much.

And then I remember 2, 5 & 10 years ago.

I recall the day when I surely said, "If not for your grace, where would I be?' because I had nothing to give.

God you've been faithful.

More than Material

I'm thankful for life, health, and strength.

Good love, because it's truly a balm.

Laughter and ingenuity from 9-year-olds.

Food that sits on my table and is seasoned well.

Amazing sister friends who lift as they climb.

New connections and broader welcoming communities.

Memories - for without them how would I know?

The old church mothers would say, "count your blessings, name them one by one."

That sticks with me today. And most days, honestly.

It's more than material.

My Earnest Prayer

Lord, strengthen the work of my hands.
Guide them into a creative space that gives your glory.
Lead them into rooms where You show up and show out.
Grow them into portals that usher in safety and sustenance.
My earnest prayer.
You're a trailblazer and I'm grateful.

Love That Repairs the Breach

For laughter.
For learning.
For friendships.
For love that repairs, covers and is given freely.
For birthdays.
For simple joys.
For newness.
For warm weather and sun and *the Son*.
We give thanks.

The Laments

lament
[luh-ment]

> *1. feelings which can show sorrow, sadness or regret.*
> *2. to mourn.*

A Lament Is a Holy Crying Out

Sometimes it's beautiful.
Sometimes it's bitter.
Yet the ground is still holy.
Sometimes it's love filled.
Sometimes it's littered with sour notes.
Everytime a lament is lifted, that space becomes holy ground.

Meet Us in the Moment They Collide

God of our joys but also our laments:

Meet us at the point where they coincide.

Sit among us in the quiet.

Breathe through us strength to be honest about where our griefs reside.

Stir in us the knowing that You're there.

Even in these things.

A Funeral Musing

While sitting in a funeral service of a dear friend, sister, and seminarian,

my grief and joy hold hands.

They sat surely alongside one another as I ushered in the reality that some healing doesn't take place in this realm.

As they sat, I felt compelled to note,

Burning my candles and wearing my good scents and eating off the china on a regular day must become a thing.

Because this all ends.

At the Intersection of Joy and Grief

God met me in my grief at a time that I was celebrating and brokenhearted, both equally.

I was joyful and sad and God sat right in the midst of it.

My wife handed me joy filled days while rubbing my back when I couldn't get out of bed because my broken heart wouldn't allow me to move.

I ate good food that nourished me and reminded me that nobody made potato salad like Aunt Mary.

God met me in my grief and allowed me to see that my joys and griefs hold hands daily.

It's in the glimmer of a song.

The way the wind whips by my face and I'll pick up a familiar scent.

Will I always idle in this intersection?

The Lament Jar Overflows

For parents who feel their best isn't enough.

For sleepless nights.

For mommy guilt and never seeming to catch up.

For kids who struggle to understand and communicate.

For caretakers who must let go.

For grief that doesn't look or feel normal.

Is this the new normal?

The jar sometimes feels overflowing.

We lament.

Holy Week Reflection

If I'm honest, Good Friday wrestles with me.

I'm yet thinking of Jesus' feelings and emotions of going to the cross.

I'm still thinking of the Disciples and how they felt knowing and unknowing of what was to come.

I'm thinking of the Mary's, his mother and his friend, and the grief they held.

I'm mourning more than a few things.

Holy Week is indeed a time of reflection.

I'll get to the joy of Sunday, soon enough.

But the feelings of Friday are heavy.

Holy Saturday

God's beloved was murdered and the world went silent.

God was silent.

The world was quiet.

Was it the grief? Did God's heart break at the death of God's son?

The silence sits with me the most.

Currently, I'm experiencing a "God is silent" moment.

It felt like days of no answer - 730 days to be exact.

It's been difficult not receiving an answer.

But Holy Saturday, a quiet Saturday doesn't mean that God is absent.

Quiet, but I know God is still there.

Resurrection Sundays

Easter service
afterwards
Mama's house
Once belonged to (my) grandparents
Ancestors felt
Cozy
Grandmama smelled like Spring time, vanilla, and sweetly
sung hymns.

Wedding earrings worn
for resurrection sunday
how befitting.
Things die
jobs
experiences
things begin anew
resurrected selves
Resurrection happens
in our everyday lives.

I Cried in a Grocery Store Parking Lot Once

Maybe if we knew that some folks cry in the grocery store parking lot before they go in to shop because this world is just tough…

And time doesn't heal all wounds.

And grief encompasses more than death.

Maybe we'd be kinder.

Maybe we'd take the cart back to the corral like a kind neighbor.

Softer.

Maybe we'd help the young mother with full hands with groceries.

Maybe we'd smile back when the cashier says hello.

Just maybe.

When the Praise Break Don't Hit

We need to hear more about grief in church.
I have sat in sanctuaries during a praise break.
Broken. Bruised. Wounded.
Not just over death.
Everything ain't praise break worthy.

Sometimes, God Does Their Best Work In Heaven

One day, we're gonna talk about the healing that only comes for someone when they transition as ancestors.

Some sickness won't be healed here.

Some hearts won't be mended here.

When we pray for healing; we have to be cognizant of the idea that some healing doesn't happen in this realm.

Sometimes, God does Their best work in heaven.

I Did Not Shift the Atmosphere, It Shifted Me

My praise did not move me out of my grief.
I didn't need my praise to do that.
I wanted answers for my grief.
My praise is what I offer and give back to God.
Why can't God hold my grief also?
My grief isn't bad.

Sometimes

Can I be thankful despite holding heavy grief?
Sometimes the clouds feel heavier than imaginable.
But absolutely I can.
Because many things can be true at the same time.
Sometimes, the answer is no answer.

Hypersensitivity Sucks

My spirit is weary.

A little transparency: I'm a lover by nature. An over-carer.

There are so many things, causes, people, etc that my heart and hands touch and want to touch some days,

I wonder if it is enough.

This IS the US

I would like to say I'm surprised.

Deep down, I am not.

This is who you are, America.

At her core, she has dirty, filthy hands.

Drenched with the blood of the people who toiled,

slaved, and died to build her.

The truth is, many people are still committed to racism, homophobia, xenophobia and misogyny; no matter how many "Black Lives Matter" and "All are welcome here" signs are put up in front windows and yards.

The truth is, many are still committed to ageism, classism, redlining and more.

This IS the US.

What Am I Doing Here?

I'm somewhere between major imposter syndrome and too much sauce because this is what I prayed for.

Let it be so.

At the End of the Day, They Will Know You By Your Love

Not by the bible verses you shared, (in context and out)
sermons you preached,
choirs you sang in,
how many tithes you paid,
or how hard you shouted.
Love IS an action word.
Your witness is in your love.

The Glue

Ask about recipes to make sure we are preserving "us."

Our people are leaving this realm and we don't have the recipes or the stories.

These things are often the glue that holds us together.

Before you gather again, I challenge you to get in the kitchen with that family member who makes that special dish like only they can.

Write the recipe down.

Record the work together.

Preserve. Preserve. Preserve.

Jaws Tight and Heavy Ladened

I'd like to unclench my jaw and breathe without feeling
heavy...
God, where is the comfort they said you'd provide?
Where is this peace they said would pass all understanding?
God, where are YOU?

The Land of Never Ending Grief

Every day I wake up and my heart is still broken.
The grief is never ending.
I grieve the years of loss
of a church community
of family turned strangers
of my cousin-sister.
Loss feels too familiar.
It's only a little easier to move with.

The Rubble Runs It

Let the ruin and rubble fill the streets like the blood we shed to build this country.

May the fury of the ancestors make way like billowing smoke.

May their spirits beset the jury forevermore.

For the Record

Jesus was here for us.
The many.
The marginalized
and folks.

Those teething on the margins.
Jesus was here for the hoes,
backsliders
and those deemed undesirable.

How Close Are You Really?

I'm wrestling with the "The Lord draws near to the broken-hearted" part of Psalms 34.

We're back and forth and back again.

I cry, but does God hear me?

My faith is tested at the weight of a God the elders say is seemingly close but feels so far away.

This love affair has felt like a battle.

When will I feel the closeness of God drawing near to my broken heart?

It's a battle for me to feel comfort from God when I am in the depths of grief.

I wonder, God will I ever know what it means to feel you near?

A Tide Doesn't Always Turn

Oh January,

You've come roaring like a lion.

Broken hearts.

Loss of loved ones.

Pain.

Even in the excitement of new beginnings, that old friend grief edges itself closer for a spot at the table.

God, remind us that our lament is holy too.

Just Get Over It, It May Not Come

You live.

You experience loss.

With deep loss, it's not something that you just get over.

a prayer of healing didn't pan out like you intended.

a call for that promotion never came.

the life you thought you'd live didn't materialize.

Grief is real even if no one physically dies.

Loss is loss.

And that hurts.

That One YEAR

Thank you. But goodbye.

You were sweet and sour simultaneously.

You were beauty and pain in concert.

You were joy and sorrow together.

I'm thankful for what you were and glad to see you leave.

2022,

You were gentle. You were kind.
You meant me to be
Well.

A Note on Loneliness In a Sea of People

A season of unintentional loneliness can be almost unbearable.

Friend groups, social events, meetings.

It's quiet even when it's loud.

I can hear the laughter and all the joy.

All I really want is to join in and engulf myself in it.

Folks dont understand it, when you seemingly have it all together.

but this.

but that.

but them.

A Moment of Transparency

Death causes me to sit in a weird space at the junction of anger and gratitude.

Just One of Those Days

Holding those of you who struggle with
getting up,
saying yes,
setting boundaries,
walking through the door,
for whatever reason in prayer,
May healing and resolve soon be your portion.

Dear God of My Wildest Dreams and Provider of All My Needs

I need a win.

I'm good for it. I'm immensely thankful. I'm really ready.

and YOU always show out.

Signed,

- a person with big goals, little coins, but is trying hard.

A Moment for the Mothers and Motherless

May today be all you want and need it to be.

If you're holding mamas and mother figures in your heart, I'm thinking of you.

If you're holding babies in your heart and not in your hands, I'm thinking of you.

If motherhood is still a hope for you, I'm thinking of you.

If motherhood isn't in the cards, I'm thinking of you..

If today is just hard, I'm holding you deeply in prayer.

Father, Can You Hear Me?

I thank God for Fathers today.

I was raised an amazing one. He's been my number one fan and cheerleader since day one.

I've been privileged to be guided by thoughtful and caring fathers.

Our village is made stronger by those who hold their jobs as fathers in high esteem.

For those holding fathers and father figures in your hearts, love to you today.

For the fathers holding children in their hearts but not their hands, love to you today.

For the fathers yet to be, love to you today.

For those whose fatherly relationships are sensitive and need additional care, love to you today.

For Those Who Stand Behind the Sacred Desk

For the wearers of the cloth.

The clergy people who will proclaim God's word.

May your words speak truth, provide comfort, and tangible ways to do justice and love mercy.

God is with you.

Remember table flipping Jesus is always an option.

Let words of your mouth and the purpose driven meditations in your heart proclaim God's goodness and glory for all who will hear.

Let it be so.

It Was Women Who First Told

For Anne Byfield, Maudine Wordlaw,Traci Blackmon, Cynthia Hale, R. Janae Pitts-Murdock, Yvette Flunder, and D. Danyelle Thomas.

For Sarah Lou Bostick, Terri Hord Owens, Anita Cobb, Christal L. Williams, and those who came before, and those who will come after.

Holding clergywomen who fight daily to be seen, heard, and understood in the pulpits and institutions they lead in my heart today.

Even though it was a woman who birthed God who would become flesh.

Even though it was a woman who yet championed for Christ as he met voices of "crucify him."

Even though it was a woman who first told of the resurrection.

My prayer for those fighting institutions who try to stifle them:

Keep preaching. Keep leading. Keep speaking truth to power, even when the words you speak causes their house of cards to crumble.

May it be so.

A Musing: Fear Based Theology

Shame or fear based theology can't do anything for me.
The God I know and love created me to be free.
That's where I'll choose to live.
In freedom.

Is It Jesus or Is It Paul?

If the truth in love conversation is thinly veiled truth in harm, I wonder if our exchanges are truth in love or are in harm.

Is it Jesus or is it Paul?

Is it Jesus or is it Harm?

Come As You Are*

The church: "Come as you are. You're fearfully and wonderfully made."

LGBTQIA people: "Ok, here I am."

Also the church: "Yeah, no, but not like that."

Also the church: "But can you arrange this song, beat these faces, sew these robes?"

Is it Jesus or is it Paul?

Is it Jesus or is it Harm?

Asking for myself.

A Musing: Love You Like I Love Paul, I Mean Jesus

Paul has become Jesus for some christians and I don't like it one bit.

Tend To Your Garden

Tend to your garden.

TEND.

TO.

YOUR GARDEN.

Feed it good things: care, love, water, boundaries.

Weed out the not so good ones: negative self talk, self hatred, imposter syndrome.

Take care in all the ways a garden needs.

There are seasons of nurturing.

There are seasons of reaping.

whatever the season.

Tend and watch it flourish.

God Can Handle It

I sit in the anger stage of grief the longest.

946 days to be exact.

I felt the rage from the moment I heard the words: "She's gone."

I heard my heartbreak when I read the words: "Thank you for you service."

I knew the world ended when I heard: "No longer welcome here."

My anger is righteous and holy.
God has to deal with me on it. God can handle this anger.

Today I Grabbed a Glimpse of You

Today I grabbed a glimpse of Patrice in the form of a hug.

She always sends me messages when I am at my loneliest points.

My person tells me often, "God is always showing you reminders of just how loved and covered you are- to remind you just how loved and covered you are."

When folks we love deeply leave this realm, it leaves a void that can't be described.

It's otherworldly to experience life without folks you once held near and dear.

But today, Patrice, I saw you. In the form of a hug from her dear friend.

I knew you crossed realms to remind me you're still here.

I knew at that moment, God knew too, I needed a glimpse of you.

I'm thankful.

God Be a Comfort

hearts are heavy and grief is abound.

wrap us in the tenderness and kindness of your love.

arm us with sweet memories that beg us to hold them close.

God be with us in our sorrows, as they walk alongside our joys.

The Joy

joy
[joi] noun/verb

1. happiness. delightfulness. overwhelmingly good.

Joy Resides Here

Joy resides here.
It takes up space. Wholly.
We must remember that in the darkest, loneliest hour.
There is a break of the day.
Joy comes in the morning.

Joy Yet Resides Here

For the Joy

Joy.
All of it.
Soaking it up.
Laying in it.
Living in it.
Rising in it.
Settling in it.
Joining in it.
Allowing it to take up more space.
Let the joy cup overflow.
All year.

A Walk Down Memory Lane

When you sit back and look at all the ways God has kept you.
Those "No's" don't feel so bad.
That fall out wasn't *that* terrible.
That reroute was a scenic blessing.
Covered and kept on all sides.
Gratitude.

Musing: Owning Your Truth

When you own your truth, no one can hold it against you.

Joy Yet Resides Here

When They Meet Me Here

I'm letting love, grace, and joy meet me here.
Who knew a one pound eight ounce preemie could come so far??
Who but God knew?
And I've been loved at every turn.
The funny thing is I haven't even truly tapped in yet.
I'm loving the journey
to me
to being better
to life
to finding joy.
May they meet me there.

They Love You

Even while grief feels like it will overpower you.

Just this day alone, you have experiences where you want to share something truly amazing with loved ones who are now ancestors.

Yet joy,

walks alongside you

reminding you that grief is where love goes when loss occurs.

God Is With Me

Emmanuel, God is with me, is the one thing that has helped me on this journey.

God if you can be near me in my joys, surely you can and will sit alongside me in my grief.

In my rage and in lack of understanding.

This is where grief and joy intersect.

God is with me.

A Balm In Indiana

If you knew all they went through,
the battles they fought.
the demons they slayed.
the prayers they prayed.
You'd might not roll your eyes so hard when they:
clap HARD for themselves.
pat themselves on the back for just getting out of bed.
finish tasks on their own timeline,
learn what self-love really looks like for them.
You never know the traumas people have lived through.
So they begin to honor self.
Ritual
Hot showers
Thick scented lotion and Vaseline ladened feet
Balms.

A Note on Growing People

It's painful, hilarious, and weird.

The process stretches you physically, mentally and spiritually.

Your uterus balloons and grows by the day.

Your brain begins to ponder all the ways you'll care for this new being.

Your spirit knows love before you've even seen a face.

But

Carrying a little person is truly evidence of God's handiwork.

I'm simply amazed.

How Great Is Our God

I love that "How great is our God" is still being sung in churches all over the world, even today.

It fills me.

It's a war cry.

It soothes a wounded spirit.

It speaks to the enemy.

It brings out the foolishness in the atmosphere.
I dare you. Speak to the storms in your life: How Great is OUR God.

Remind Them

To all who stand behind the sacred desk this morning.

Remind them: Jesus was a brown man murdered by the state.

Remind them: Jesus was a table flipping man who broke the chains of the status quo.

Remind them: radical love means no more turning a blind eye.

Remind them: thoughts and prayers are great but action is needed.

Let God rest, rule, and abide today.

I Write to Remind You

God always uses the month of February to jumpstart my heart and remind me that my ground is fertile because I tend to it.

There is something about the 28 days of a month dedicated to Black history, excellence, and change makers that gets my wheels geared up for the year.

It helps me set the pace for the coming planting season.

My garden starts with energized soil.

I dig out the rocks.

I weed through the clay.

I water the soil.

I feed it good things.

I Can Only Imagine

Imagine kids growing up to do exactly what they were created to do.

Be their own person

But if there were ever a question,

Love lives here.

The people in the spaces I reside in will be

loved

supported

and affirmed at every stage.

In a cold harsh and unrelenting world, this will be a safe space.

joy will reside here.

A Love Handed Down

There was a love handed down by Big mama via grocery store lists written on torn envelopes in dainty cursive writing,

in the crinkles of Oil of Olay laden hands, and Crisco covered arms.

Hips that swayed to spirit filled hymns and

rouge colored lips, and stomachs smoothed with tight girdles ready for church mornings and

hands that passed jars filled with pot likker from greens grown in backyards, and

magic made with secret handslips of a twenty through your fingers for good measure.

There was a love handed down.

Now that love stretches to the depths of the Earth and calls back as an ancestor.

This love rocks me while I sleep and calls me to remember.

A love so grand and pure keeps me in ways I don't always understand.

Monumental love,

sustained.

A Musing: A Few Things I Know to Be True

God is kind.

Faith + Therapy are working together for the good of me because I do love the Lord.

Healing is not linear.

Laughter is indeed medicine.

Funeral chicken, baby shower meatballs, and church punch are a holy trifecta of celebration food.

We deserve the things:

good things,

safe things,

healthy thing.

a kept life

Oh, to be kept
by God
by the love from a wife
by the laugher of a daughter
by the prayers of a mother
by the connection of a sister
by the goodness of friends.
39 hits different.
Body changed.
Life transitioned.
Isolation. Elevation.
Challenges. Joys.
But God always sees fit to show up in beautiful and bountiful
ways.
Oh, to be kept.

Doing the Work and Putting the Work On It

Going boldly toward my dreams wasn't always easy.

But I decided that:

Doing the work, making intentions, and putting a prayer on it were my best course of action.

And once I did my part, I came to know:

The universe *is* conspiring to see my dreams come to fruition.

a love letter to the Black Women who love me well

Black women love me well.

They are the hand I fan with.

The joy that holds me.

Black women pull me in and close and sit with me when I'm in need of care.

They're the thread that stitches me together and keeps me from crumbling.

The gifts that give me more than I could've ever imagined.

Black women are magic to me.

The embodiment of what staying the course and leaning in looks like.

They fill my cup and it runs over and some.

I am because they are.

I am forever indebted to Black women for the ways they keep me.

That Moment When

prayer,
praise,
patience,
& preparation meet or
Godfidence.

If I Told You All the Places God Met Me

Let me tell you of all the places where God has whispered to
me.
Let me tell you of all the ways that God shows up in ways
that don't look holy.
Let me tell you about some of the places where God has
called my name.
Let me tell you about the ways God shows up in a secular
song.

I felt the breath of God in the whisper of the wind.
I felt the care of God while a swag and surf occurred at a
college campus party.
I answered back on a city bus praying I made it to my
destination safely.
I knew God knew my name when a songwriter sang, "Will
you believe in love and the promise that it gives?"

If I told you all of the places where God met me, would you
take my word for it?

Joy Yet Resides Here

Clap for Yourself, You Deserve

Because... getting out of bed,
self love,
making progress,
saying no,
graduations,
promotions,
new homes,
new businesses,
and holidays.
Can all be a lot to digest.
CLAP HARD FOR YOURSELF.
for the moments you made it over,
the days you pushed through,
the mountains you climbed and then some.
I'm clapping hard for us too.
Even as the tears flow.
God be with us as we cheer.

Gratitude Ain't Even the Half

I could've and likely should've lost my mind.

The level of being kept by God

who sees me, and calls me by name and claims me as Their own,

and my loves

who allow me to operate in my gifting without having to dim my light,

and the ancestors

which guide my path and cloak me in care from the otherside.

These truths live rent free in my head.

Gratitude ain't even the half of it.

Joy Yet Resides Here

Restoring the Years

For 2022, 2023, 2024 and beyond:
Joy.
All of it.
Soaking it up.
Laying in it.
Living in it.
Rising in it.
All year.

A Musing: Good Love Is Balm

Good love is balm.
A soothing agent.
A medicine.
A corrector.
It is a solace.
It is a peacemaker.
It is a safe place to land.
Whether it be platonic, familial or romantic.
Good, safe, affirming love is necessary.

Good Love and a Promise Kept

When Toni Morrison said, "She didn't fall in love, she rose in it," it sat with me.

Once I was in a place to know what rising in love felt like, I felt it deep in my bones.

It lived with me.

There's something to be said about rising and carrying love with, alongside, and within you.

And rise is what we've done.

We've seen some things.

We've laughed, cried, had scary moments, prayed, been mad, been vulnerable, and made sure to laugh again.

Loving you and rising in love with you has been one of the bravest things I've ever done.

Ask me and I'll do it all over again.

Good love and a promise kept.

This is my story, this is my song.

Musings: Pride Month

Sometimes the bravest thing you can do is show up as yourself, for yourself.

I'm privileged to get to show up colorful doing life in intentional love with my partner.

One of the bravest things I've ever done was shown up as me in the honoring of us.

Sometimes pride moments are deeper than parades, parties, and love is love quotes.

Sometimes, it's finally honoring the self you've always known.

So for those of you who:

may not always walk in society's straight lines,

support those who march to the beat of colorful drums,

parent or neighbor with someone in the LGBTQIA+ family,

believe that love is love and love is good,

honor the humanity of people and all our variables.

I see you. You can show up. You belong.

A Note on Motherhood When the Dreams Are More than Enough

For the mothers who dream while living the mom life, it's possible, keep going.

For the mom who works long after the babies are in bed, you're amazing.

For the mama who does it all and then some, I see you.

Final Musing: To Self

A girls girl.

Friend to funny folks.

Lover of the outlier.

Singer.

Spice slanger.

Writer.

Mama.

Wife.

Podcaster.

Groupie of table flipping Jesus.

Joy Yet Resides Here

Joy Will Reside: Here

It may not be perfect, but it's a great life.
A life gifted to me.
To love.
To sow good things.
To give plenty.
Thankful.

Joy resides here.

Acknowledgements

I want to thank God in their never ending love and devotion to me. God, I see you and I'm glad you call me friend.

To the VK Press Team:
Thank you, God dreams.

Shavonne, you're a joy to work with. Thank you for pushing and pushing and pulling and pulling. But also loving the book to life.

JY, You are a gift to this world and I'm thankful I got to know you starting way back at The House. From Midtown to the moon!

Tania, you're an incredible artist. Thank you for your gifts and willingness to say yes.

Ess, what an incredible artist you are. The world is richly blessed with your art residing in it. Thank you!

To my wife, Sissy, you've been a friend to me while I became a better friend to pen. Thank you for your affirming love. Always. All ways.

To Ms. Maddie, my girl, you're a world changer. Thank you for always showing mommy a better way.

To Daddy, Mom and Camylle, Thank you for the ways you love me. Thanks for always letting me be.

To the Tribe, I'm surrounded by a group of women who sharpen me and give me back the most incredible love. Thanks for loving me back the long way.

To the reader, thank you for being here. I believe our lives were supposed to connect this way. Just you holding this book is balm to my soul. Thank you.

About The Author

Candace Boyd Simmons is a Midwestern based award winning, multi-genre creative. Born and raised in Indiana, Candace writes to give herself freedom. Often found writing about food, via FoodLoveTog.com she combines her love of all things food with nearly 20 years of marketing and non-profit professional experience.

Her multifaceted creative space which thrives on food creativity. Candace has become a sought after leader in the blogging, food education, food creative space. Known in the Indianapolis community as "The Spice Slanger," sharing her love of cooking and leaving no dish unseasoned is what she's all about. Find her in community as co-host of the award-winning podcast *Black Girls Eating* or shaking tables as an anti-racism trainer or seasoning the masses with her handcrafted spiceline.

Candace resides in her hometown of Indianapolis with her wife and daughter. In her free time, she cooks, jokes and watches reruns of *A Different World*. She's passionate about food security and access. Candace is currently a Master of Divinity (M.Div) and Theological Studies (MTS) candidate at Christian Theological Seminary. Most of all, Candace believes that our joys and our grief must hold hands. She believes good love is balm, and that God is always here for the folks who reside in the margins.

Her first book, *Joy Yet Resides Here*, was released by VK Press in 2025. Her next written project, a devotional, is forthcoming.

Connect with Candace online at candacebsimmons.com or on any social media platform at @kendence and @foodlovetog.